Original title:
Pinecone Punchlines

Copyright © 2025 Creative Arts Management OÜ
All rights reserved.

Author: Penelope Hawthorne
ISBN HARDBACK: 978-1-80567-429-0
ISBN PAPERBACK: 978-1-80567-728-4

Jestful Needles

In the forest, a joke was spun,
A tree wore a hat and said, "I'm done!"
The squirrels all chuckled with cheer,
As branches waved high, from far and near.

The fox told a tale, quite absurd,
About a chirping, singing bird.
"She tried to dance, fell flat on her face,
Now wiggles in wind, in silly grace."

The Chuckling Grove

In a grove where laughter resides,
Trees wear smiles, they cannot hide.
A raccoon did cartwheels, round and round,
While the owls hooted, oh what a sound!

Mice shared puns, fluffed their tails bright,
Jokes bounced like acorns, pure delight.
The moon peeked in, with a twinkling eye,
"Tell me a secret, oh, don't be shy!"

Pine Bough Banter

Beneath the boughs, old tales unfold,
Of a porcupine who was daringly bold.
He wore a tux that was all out of style,
Said, "I'm dressed for the party, stay a while!"

A chipmunk chimed in, with a grin so wide,
"Why not wear stripes, instead of just pride?"
Leaves rustled with glee, as giggles erupted,
Nature's own humor, impeccably cupped!

Giggles in the Pines

In the pines, a gathering took place,
With laughter and joy, a funny embrace.
A beaver with glasses cracked a good one,
"I'm working on my dam, but I'm really just fun!"

The breeze tickled ears, floated far and wide,
Jokes slipped like sap as the critters abide.
The sun set low, a golden glow,
In the heart of the woods, where chuckles flow!

Sprouted Smiles

In the forest where giggles grow,
Trees whisper jokes to the brook below.
Squirrels chuckle and race in delight,
While sunbeams dance and take flight.

A rabbit hops, with a twinkle in his eye,
As butterflies flutter, dancing high.
Every rustle brings laughter anew,
Nature's comedy, a perfect view.

The Playful Pines

Beneath the pines where laughter rings,
Funny shadows dance and sing.
A woodpecker tapping, making a beat,
While a chipmunk juggles, oh what a feat!

The breeze tells tales, swaying each branch,
As critters join in a whimsical dance.
Even the rocks wear silly grins,
In this forest where humor spins.

Nature's Laughing Stock

Oh, the punchlines that nature conceals,
In every rustling leaf, laughter reveals.
A deer trips over its own two hooves,
While a crow caws out, making the moves.

With acorns dropping, a comical sound,
Mushrooms sprout up, looking around.
Every squirrel seems to have a plan,
In the wild, we all share a laugh, oh man!

Arboreal Anecdotes

Underneath the towering trees,
Whispers of jest float on the breeze.
A raccoon sneezes, it's quite a scene,
As grasshoppers leap, dressed in green.

Little critters gather, tales to spin,
Stories of mischief cause them to grin.
With every flicker of tail and cheer,
Nature's comedy is always near.

The Poetry of Pine Fronds

In the shade where laughter grows,
Corniest jokes the forest knows.
Each frond a giggle, sways just so,
Tickling toes of those below.

Whispers dance through needle sights,
As squirrels plot their comedy nights.
With acorns as their props on stage,
They take a bow at every age.

Nutty Nonsense

A chipmunk wearing a tiny hat,
Says, "How's that for a silly spat?"
He juggles nuts with a wink and grin,
While rabbits cheer, 'Let the fun begin!'

The owl hoots jokes like a stand-up pro,
While deer and raccoons line up in a row.
Nature's laughter fills the air,
As critters roll, without a care.

Laughter Down the Trail

On the winding path, merry tunes,
Echo through the trees and dunes.
With every step, a chuckle spry,
As playful shadows dance nearby.

A fox tells tales of silly stunts,
While bears join in with hearty grunts.
Each leaf a laugh, each twig a tease,
The trail of giggles aims to please.

Forest Fables and Frivolities

Once a frog, quite proud of his croak,
Declared himself the king of joke.
With every ribbit, he stole the show,
Making all the critters glow.

A wise old tree chuckled with glee,
As laughter rang through the canopy.
In flurries of fun, the tales unfold,
In a forest where mirth is gold.

The Forest's Secret Humor

In the wood, where shadows play,
Trees chuckle in a breezy sway.
A squirrel's joke, oh what a sight,
Makes the sunbeam giggle bright.

Underneath a leafy bow,
Fungi laugh with silent vow.
A rabbit trips, the deer just stare,
Nature laughs, beyond compare.

Little ants in a conga line,
Dance around, oh how they shine!
The owl hoots, a witty bird,
Spreading jokes, so absurd.

When nightfall comes, the crickets tease,
Telling tales of summer breeze.
The moonlight glints with twinkly glee,
Even stars find humor free.

Conical Capers

Round and round the forest spins,
Where the laughter truly begins.
A hedgehog rolls, slips on a twig,
Ends up stuck, what a funny gig!

Tall pine trees lead a silly dance,
Branches swaying in a prancing chance.
Beneath them lies that precious stash,
Nutty giggles, in a flash!

Owls wear glasses, wise and bright,
Swapping tales by moon's soft light.
A joke or two, they share in fun,
With each hoot, the laughter's spun.

In this woodland, joy's the prize,
Capering critters, full of surprise.
With every rustle, there's a pun,
Nature's humor, never done!

Eclectic Forest Giggles

The trees have friends, both big and small,
Chirpy birds and bugs that crawl.
Each day they gossip, what a crew,
Their laughter spreads, a merry brew.

A beaver builds, but oh, he slips,
Down the bank, he takes some trips.
With a splash, the frogs all croak,
Ribbiting jokes, what a hoax!

The butterflies ?wear mismatched socks,
Flitting 'round, they dodge the rocks.
Buzzing bees with funny hats,
Join the party, pitter-pats!

Under the stars, a riot unfolds,
Dreams of laughter, joys retold.
In this forest, giggles thrive,
Beneath the canopies, joy's alive!

Cone-shaped Whimsy

Look at the cones, so round and neat,
Gathering smiles, quite a feat!
They joke and tumble all around,
Creating laughter, joy abound.

The squirrels race, a nutty spree,
Tripping on roots, oh can't you see?
With every slip, a chorus sounds,
Of chuckles bright, from leafy grounds.

The moonlight glows, casting shadows,
Where giggling pixies share their woes.
They whisper tales of joy and cheer,
Enchanting all who happen near.

In this whimsical, cone-shaped land,
Giggles echo, laughter, quite grand.
Each whispering breeze is filled with cheer,
As the forest's humor draws us near.

Cheerful Cast of Conifers

In a forest where saplings jest,
Laughter echoes, a nature fest.
Trees giggle in the breezy air,
While squirrels dance without a care.

Needles point with a teasing flair,
Branches sway like they're unaware.
Pines tell jokes to the passing deer,
With every chuckle, the sun draws near.

Breezes tickle each leafy friend,
A comedy show that won't soon end.
The woods are staged, the audience wide,
Nature's humor, a joyful ride.

So come and witness this lively plot,
Where trees are jesters and all is hot.
Every rustle, a punchline served,
In this merry land, no love reserved.

Slapstick in the Pines

In the heart of the timbered scene,
Bumbling bears get caught in between.
Branches trip on a sneaky breeze,
As critters frolic with utmost ease.

A raccoon slips, what a grand fall,
Right into a pile that won't seem small.
He shakes off leaves with a bob and a spin,
And giggles as friends join in the din.

Chipmunks hop on a slippery log,
While owls roll their eyes at the smog.
Each twig bends as laughter sways,
In this vibrant dance where nature plays.

So bring your joy to this forest bright,
Where humor shines with pure delight.
In the pines, every stumble or slip,
Is just a part of the laughter trip.

Nature's Comedic Interlude

In the glade where shadows play,
A woodpecker cracks jokes all day.
Squirrels chuckle at acorn schemes,
While breezes carry hilarious dreams.

Each rustling leaf tells secrets dear,
A mouse spins tales that all can hear.
In this patch of green and gold,
Every creature's got humor bold.

Mushrooms giggle, what a sight!
Under moonbeams, they share the light.
The night critters join in a song,
Making moments where all belong.

So join the fun, let laughter bloom,
In cozy corners, there's always room.
Nature's comedy, a joyful spree,
Bringing smiles for you and me.

Amusing Acorns

Acorns roll, they run, they hide,
Playing games with the wind as guide.
Each little nut a comedian bold,
With stories of mischief waiting to unfold.

They tumble and trip in a merry race,
As squirrels chase them with silly face.
Laughter erupts from the leafy shade,
In this grand act, no pranks will fade.

Fungi cheer as they pass by,
With humorous quips that amplify.
Nature's laughter, a sweet refrain,
Echoing joy in each tiny grain.

So watch the stage where the acorns play,
A circus of fun in a woodland ballet.
With each giggle, more magic grows,
As nature's humor softly flows.

The Amused Arboretum

In the grove where whispers play,
Trees wear smiles, light as spray.
Squirrels giggle, hiding nuts,
While branches sway and do their cuts.

Each branch jests with leaves in glee,
I saw a tree dance, can you see?
Bark makes jokes; it's quite absurd,
Nature's laughter, in every word.

Fungi reach for a tickling spree,
Mushrooms laugh, oh so carefree.
Breezes carry each cheeky quip,
With every swaying, a comic flip.

Even the roots are a hearty bunch,
Fooling around at the base of brunch.
So come and join the leafy jest,
In this woodland where humor is best.

Pine Tree Puns

What did the pine say to the fir?
You're looking sharp; that's for sure!
With every breeze, a new wisecrack,
They share their jokes; nothing they lack.

The needles whisper cheeky rhymes,
Cracking up through forest climes.
When it rains, they snicker bright,
Pine humor shines in every light.

When cones come down, it's time to laugh,
Sharing tales of treecraft gaffes.
Spruce gets punny in its own way,
Bringing joy to every day.

So take a stroll without a frown,
Let tree humor turn it around.
Among the pines, where laughter rings,
Life's a joke; oh, what it brings!

Woodland Chuckle Fest

Under the canopy, laughter roams,
With every critter; it finds homes.
Raccoons tell tall tales at night,
While owls hoot, a comedic plight.

Bunnies hop with a cheeky grin,
Sharing whispers of where they've been.
With every burrow, a punchline grows,
Nature's humor, everyone knows.

The brook chuckles, a bubbly cheer,
Rippling jokes for all to hear.
Cicadas play rhythms, so spry,
A symphony of laughter in the sky.

Join the fest; feel the delight,
In wooded realms where fun takes flight.
With every rustle, a giggle's near,
Woodland chuckles, forever dear.

The Humor of Nature's Crafts

In nature's workshop, funny things,
Woodpeckers drill, creating rings.
Branches twist in cunning ways,
As trees fashion jokes for days.

The acorns roll like tiny clowns,
Telling tales in leafy gowns.
With humor woven into vines,
Each leaf seems to hold punchlines.

Bees buzz jokes from flower to flower,
Sharing laughter in sunlit hour.
While dewdrops giggle on a petal's edge,
Nature crafts humor; such a pledge!

So when you wander through the green,
Listen for laughter; it's a scene.
In every leaf, a story lasts,
From the humor of nature's crafts.

Whimsy in the Woods

In the woods where shadows play,
Squirrels dance through bright array.
A chipmunk juggles acorn treats,
With laughter ringing through the fleets.

Trees chuckle in the gentle breeze,
While rabbits hop with giggles, please.
A bear shares jokes with honey bees,
Creating smiles with such ease.

A fox in glasses reads a book,
While every critter stops to look.
They laugh at tales, both wild and grand,
As nature's jesters take the stand.

In whimsy's grasp, the forest thrives,
With silly antics, joy derives.
A heart lightens, worries cease,
In this playful woodland peace.

Jests Under the Pines

Under pines where shadows twirl,
A wise old owl gives jokes a whirl.
He winks his eye, delivers puns,
As all the creatures hoot with fun.

A raccoon tells a tale so sly,
About the night he dared to fly.
His friends just roll with comic ease,
As laughter dances through the trees.

The deer clap hooves at clever tricks,
While foxes giggle, sharing licks.
The laughter rings like sweet chimes sound,
In this wild haven, joy is found.

Beneath the stars, where spirits soar,
Each punchline opens up the door.
To joy—a gift, where all align,
With jests and giggles, under pines.

Cone-shaped Stories

Gather 'round, the tales begin,
Of quirky critters and their kin.
A hedgehog spins a yarn of fame,
While mockingbirds chant out his name.

With every twist, the laughter grows,
As pinecones crack with silly woes.
A turtle slips, a dizzy dance,
His friends all gasp, then break in prance.

A beaver builds a wobbly wall,
It sways and tips, then takes a fall.
The forest erupts in joyous mirth,
As tales unfold of pinecone worth.

Each story shared brings laughter bright,
As woodland friends unite with light.
In cone-shaped dreams where humor reigns,
The heart delights, the joy remains.

Sylvan Snickers

In the glade where whispers talk,
A wily fox takes his evening walk.
He cracks a joke about the rain,
While squirrels giggle, spry and vain.

A porcupine, with quills so sharp,
Plays the banjo, strumming a lark.
Each pluck brings out a fit of cheer,
Echoing far for all to hear.

A badger's on a soapbox high,
With witticisms that lift the sky.
The woodland giggles in delight,
As he spins tales into the night.

With every chuckle, spirits rise,
In sylvan snickers, laughter flies.
In this embrace of nature's jest,
Every heart feels truly blessed.

Laughter Among Conifers

In the forest, jokes take flight,
Trees whisper laughter in the night.
Squirrels gather with their snacks,
Cracking jokes, no time to relax.

Bark breaks into giggles and glee,
Branches sway like a comedy spree.
Raccoons roll on the forest floor,
Telling tales that leave us wanting more.

The chipmunks trade puns without care,
While owls hoot with a wise old flair.
Each twist of nature brings a chuckle,
In this grove, no one's a knuckle.

Even the shadows begin to dance,
As laughter echoes, a joyous trance.
With every branch, a grin aligns,
A playful romp 'neath towering pines.

Spruce Smirks in the Breeze

Under spruces, a bit of fun,
Joking safely away from the sun.
Ferns sway with a comedic nod,
Tickling toes like a playful prod.

The pine needles drop, sharing laughs,
As rabbits hop with comical gaffes.
A bear joins in with a sly little grin,
Making all woodland creatures spin.

Squirrels tell tales of acorn heists,
While deer giggle at wild mushroom feasts.
In this vibrant leafy bazaar,
Every jest shines like a star.

The breeze carries laughter to the sky,
Nature's punchlines float and fly.
With each gust, a cheerful embrace,
Spruce trees chuckle in this wild space.

Chuckles From the Canopy

High above, the branches sway,
Hosting jokes in a leafy café.
With whispers and giggles, they convene,
Creating laughter, a joyful machine.

Parrots squawk with clever wit,
While monkeys swing, refusing to sit.
The canopy erupts in playful sound,
As humor flows freely all around.

Caterpillars laugh at their slow pace,
While butterflies flutter, a colorful race.
They tease the winds that try to mime,
In this treetop world, it's always prime.

Laughter echoes through the pine,
A chorus of whimsy, so divine.
In the trees where the fun must reign,
Every chuckle is nature's gain.

Treetop Tickles

In the treetops, giggles grow,
Like playful breezes that softly flow.
Every twig a slapstick line,
Nature's laughter, so sweetly divine.

The woodpecker drums a hilarious tune,
While raccoons plan pranks under the moon.
Each squirrel snickers, sharing a glance,
As the whole forest joins in a dance.

Fluffy clouds drift, joining the fun,
Casting shadows where laughter is spun.
A chorus of critters, no pause in sight,
Treetop tickles whisper pure delight.

From conifer heights, the jests take flight,
In this green comedy, hearts feel light.
With every chuckle, a joy so fine,
The laughter continues, forever entwined.

The Quirk of Evergreen Quips

In the forest, laughter swells,
Trees swap stories, oh what spells!
Squirrels chuckle in the trees,
Telling tales with utmost ease.

A wise old oak, with bark so deep,
Whispers jokes that make us leap.
Witty jabs from roots below,
Nature's jesters steal the show.

Pines point fingers at the ash,
Making fun, it's quite a bash!
Raccoons join in with their glee,
Dancing 'round as wild as can be.

So next time you walk in the wood,
Listen close, it's all quite good!
The trees have secrets, fun to share,
A quirky world beyond compare.

Jest in the Juniper

In junipers, where laughter grows,
Beneath the boughs, the humor flows.
Tiny birds tease with their chirps,
Cracking jokes that make us smirks.

A chipmunk with a witty grin,
Spins a tale of where he's been.
He tickles leaves and shakes the trees,
Don't take life too seriously, please!

The sage-brush chuckles softly there,
As shadows play, we dance with flair.
Laughter echoes through the glade,
In nature's arms, all worries fade.

With every rustle and little sound,
Joy in the junipers can be found.
So come along, and join the fun,
In this woodland, smiles weigh a ton.

Laughter Among the Larch

Beneath the larch, where giggles bloom,
A playful mood fills up the room.
The wind carries a jolly tune,
As we laugh beneath the moon.

Playful shadows dance around,
Nature's games, a joyful sound.
A woodpecker, with a quick tap,
Shares a punchline in his rap.

The forest floor, a stage to roam,
Every tree calls it a home.
With silly pranks and bright-eyed schemes,
We weave together our wild dreams.

So let us roll among the pine,
With laughter sweet like vintage wine.
In every stride, let joy impart,
A symphony of nature's heart.

Sylvan Satire Unfolds

In the cool shade, the satire flies,
Boughs above whisper clever sighs.
Every leaf with a joke to spill,
Nature's humor, a funny thrill.

The fox, oh sly, with antics grand,
Steals the show from where he stands.
He plays tricks and tells his tales,
Among the roots where laughter hails.

Frolicking hare with a wink and jest,
Makes even the grumpiest crow jest.
With every hop and playful spin,
The forest laughs, it's where we begin.

So gather 'round, let laughter reign,
In this grove, we'll dance like rain.
With woodland humor, funny and bright,
Together we'll share delight every night.

Laughter in the Thicket

In the thicket where critters play,
A squirrel danced on a bright, sunny day.
He slipped on a nut, fell right on his back,
And landed in leaves with a comical clack.

The rabbits all giggled, the birds sang a tune,
As the poor squirrel hopped up, howling at the moon.
With a twist and a turn, he claimed it was fate,
As he tried to impress all his friends on a plate.

"Who needs acorns?" he shouted with glee,
"When you've got moves that are funky like me!"
The thicket erupted with laughter and cheer,
As that little nut dancer spread joy far and near.

Every tumble and wiggle, a lesson to see,
That silliness always makes friends, you agree?
So join in the fun, as the day drifts away,
In the thicket of laughter, let's sing and not sway.

Cone Chronicles

A pine tree stood regal, with cones all around,
Each one a story, waiting to be found.
A chipmunk named Chuck had a jest up his sleeve,
He crafted a tale that no one would believe.

"I once met a pinecone who fancied itself smart,
It wore little glasses and played the fine art."
The woodland folks chuckled, their sides all a'aching,
As Chuck spun his yarn, laughter never breaking.

Then along came a crow, cawing loud from a limb,
"Those cones might be funny, but I think they're quite grim!
For every time I try to perch for a look,
I end up with sap that makes me a rook!"

The animals rallied, uniting their quips,
With every new punchline, they doubled their grips.
For in cone-laden forests where humor does sprout,
Every laugh is a treasure, without any doubt.

Hilarity in the Hemlocks

Underneath hemlocks, where shadows do dance,
The raccoons debated, and fate took a chance.
One claimed to be stealthy, as quiet as air,
While the others erupted, with laughter to share.

"Stealthy!" they howled, "You mean clumsy and loud,
With your wobbly waddle, you'll never be proud!"
But the raccoon just winked, with a grin so wide,
"Sometimes it's best to enjoy the fun ride."

They launched into games of hide and seek fast,
With missteps and giggles, they hoped it would last.
But one poor raccoon fell right into the stream,
His friends roared with laughter, they couldn't help but beam!

"Now that's a new splash! Did you bring us a prize?"
They teased him with glee, as he dried off with sighs.
In the hemlocks' embrace, where humor runs free,
Each mishap brings joy, like a leaf on a spree.

The Jolly Juniper

In a grove of junipers, life's jolly and bright,
The critters all gathered, ready for laughter's flight.
With a fox named Felix, and an owl named Claire,
They plotted some jokes to tickle the air.

Felix pulled out a riddle, sharp as a whip,
"What's soft as a feather but can give you a trip?"
The junipers rustled as laughter took wing,
When the answer was "clouds!" the whole glade would sing.

Then Claire, in her wisdom, hooted out loud,
"Why was the juniper such a proud crowd?"
They waited with giggles; she answered with flair,
"Because it could root for its friends everywhere!"

With each little pun, the day sparkled bright,
Juniper joy spread, a wonderful sight.
So gather your friends, let the chuckles ignite,
For in jolly junipers, laughter takes flight.

Nature's Nods and Nonsense

In the forest where laughter grows,
Trees wear smiles, it surely shows.
A squirrel trips on a crooked twig,
And giggles burst, oh what a jig!

Frogs play leapfrog like champions bold,
While chatter echoes, stories told.
Breezes dance with a cheeky grin,
Nature's banter, let the fun begin!

Bouncing berries roll with glee,
Chatting mushrooms, oh can't you see?
Whimsical winds whisper light,
Joyful antics take their flight!

Laughter spills from roots so deep,
In this forest, secrets keep.
Nature's jokes bloom all day,
In each shadow, laughter plays.

Snickers of the Spruce

Spruce trees giggle in the breeze,
Tickling branches with such ease.
Pine needles whisper silly tales,
As playful shadows dance and sail.

A bobcat sneezes, what a sound!
Fluffy owls spin round and round.
Raccoons caught in a silly plight,
Bouncing through the moonlit night.

Chipmunks chuckle, sharing cheer,
As nature's jokes flow crystal clear.
The sun winks down with plenty of fun,
While breezes play, the day's not done!

In the arboreal circus here,
Giggles echo, no trace of fear.
A running stream joins in the jest,
Nature's laughter feels the best!

Fables from the Pine Frond

Underneath the massive limbs,
Raccoons tell tales of their whims.
A wise old owl with a cheeky smile,
Shares fables from the pine, all the while.

A dancing deer with rhythm divine,
Joined the jesters beneath the pine.
Frogs in tuxedos croak their regret,
As shoes get muddy, yet no one's upset.

Bouncing bunny, with jokes galore,
Tells of adventures and much more.
With every chuckle, the forest beams,
In a world alive with whimsical dreams.

Laughter flows from leaf to leaf,
Nature's humor, beyond belief.
In this realm rich with delight,
Every day is a comic sight.

Tall Tales Under Tall Trees

Beneath the pines, tall tales unfurl,
A story told with a playful swirl.
A beaver with a hat and a grin,
Paddles along with mischief within.

An acorn slips, it lands with flair,
Causing giggles in the crisp air.
Foxes in coats of vibrant hue,
Share laughter and puns 'til the night is through.

A turtle jigs with a jazzy beat,
While dapper ducks dance on their feet.
Each creature adds to the jolly scene,
Under tall trees, full of sheen.

All around, the chorus grows,
Nature's humor shoots like arrows.
Together we share each hearty cheer,
Underneath the canopy, joy is near.

Humor in the Hushed Grove

In the silence, a rustle, a curious sight,
An acorn dressed up, it's quite a delight.
Squirrels chuckle in coats made of bark,
While a bird tries to dance, but misses its mark.

The wise old owl hoots jokes to the crowd,
As chipmunks giggle, growing quite loud.
Fungi in funny hats start to appear,
Smiling at all, spreading good cheer.

Secret giggles in leafy embrace,
The woodpecker's peck is a rhythmic bass.
A rabbit with shades tries to look cool,
Jumping around like it's nobody's fool.

Nature's comedy show, no tickets to buy,
Just laughter and joy under the sky.
In the spongy soft moss, lay your head low,
The humorous tales of the forest will flow.

Spiky Laughs of the Forest

In the shade of the trees where the laughter explodes,
A hedgehog tells tales as he strolls down the roads.
With prickles so sharp, yet a heart that's so kind,
He jokes with the leaves, leaving troubles behind.

High up in the boughs, the parrots compete,
With voices so silly, they can't find their beat.
One squawks a pun as the others all cheer,
Echoing laughter that all creatures can hear.

Down by the stream, the frogs leap with flair,
One croaks a pun, causing others to stare.
The fish roll their eyes, splashing with mirth,
As the sun sets the stage, brightening the earth.

Nature's own circus, an endless delight,
With critters all laughing, oh what a sight!
So come to the woods, where the fun never wanes,
In spiky, sweet spaces, let humor reign.

Chuckles Beneath the Boughs

Underneath branches, the giggles take flight,
A raccoon in glasses reads jokes every night.
The moon takes a peek, with a grin that's wide,
While fireflies dance, full of joy, side by side.

A porcupine whispers, "What's your favorite tree?"
"I pine for the jokes, come and laugh with me!"
The laughter rolls out with the breeze up above,
Each creature together, united by love.

Beneath tangled vines, a picnic of fun,
With berries so juicy, there's plenty to run.
The shadows all wiggle, the grass starts to sway,
As the punchlines emerge at the end of the day.

So join in the chorus, from dusk until dawn,
In the nooks of the grove, we'll keep laughing on.
With chuckles and smiles, the forest's our muse,
Let's celebrate joy in the paths that we choose.

The Conical Comedy

In the heart of the woods where the tall trees lean,
Lies a stage made of cones, oh what a scene!
The squirrels take notes, they're the star of the show,
With antics and acorns, they steal the tableau.

A fox dons a hat, looking sharp as a tack,
Says, "Why was the tree in the schoolyard so whack?"
"It couldn't find its roots, it was waving too high!"
The chuckles erupt, even clouds start to cry.

With a circle of friends, each branch holds their breath,
As the pine needles whisper, "We'll laugh until death!"
The punchlines fly by, like leaves in the air,
Spreading sweet joy, no worries or care.

So gather your pals, let the nature show start,
With a conical twist and a merry heart.
In the forest, the humor binds every tree,
In laughter we sing, forever carefree.

Ticklish Bark

In the woods, the trees do shake,
A ticklish laugh, a funny quake.
Squirrels giggle, they dance and twirl,
With laughter echoing, flags unfurl.

Branches sway with a lively glee,
The forest whispers, 'Come laugh with me!'
A rustle here, a chuckle there,
Beneath the boughs, it's a comical fair.

Leaves exchange their silly jokes,
While acorns roll like little folks.
The wind joins in with a playful howl,
Nature's jesters, taking a bow.

Through laughter's woods, we'll wander ways,
As bark and buzz bring joyful rays.
So let us roam where humor thrives,
In the ticklish forests, where joy arrives.

Hoots and Hollers From the Pines

Up in the branches, the wise owls hoot,
With feathers fluffed, a whimsical suit.
They share tall tales of tree-top lore,
And tumble down with a hearty roar.

Creaking limbs make the funniest sounds,
As laughter bounces around the grounds.
The pines erupt with keening glee,
Each holler a note in the woodland spree.

Birds chirp songs so hilariously bright,
As shadows dance in the golden light.
A raccoon waves, with a mischievous grin,
Inviting all to the fun within.

Nature's orchestra plays the most jolly tune,
While critters make mischief 'neath the full moon.
So join the chorus, let joy take flight,
With hoots and hollers, our spirits ignite.

The Merry Memory of Saplings

Little saplings sway with a nod,
Recalling tales of deeds quite odd.
They whisper stories of times gone by,
With chuckles woven in each sigh.

Their roots, they dance in the soil's embrace,
As playful breezes spin in the space.
Each leaf a giggle shared in fun,
With sunny laughter when day is done.

The seedlings tease about growing tall,
In friendly jests, they challenge all.
"Who grows fastest?" they giggle and cheer,
As they grow round, taller each year.

Sprouts beam bright with nature's humor,
As sunshine gives their laughter room.
In memory of days filled with cheer,
Saplings hold joy forever near.

A Pine's Jest

A pine stands tall, with a playful grin,
Ready to share a tale from within.
He shakes his needles, does a little jig,
Drawing in smiles, oh so big.

Jests flutter down like the pinecone rain,
Bouncing off rocks and giggling again.
"Why did the squirrel cross the road?"
"To get to the nuts"—the punchline flowed.

Branches waggle with each punchline,
While critters join in, feeling fine.
The forest echoes with glee-filled roars,
As laughter spills through open doors.

So gather 'round, hear the pine's wise jest,
Nature's humor is simply the best.
With trees and critters joining the fun,
In the laughter-rich woods, joy's never done.

Forest Frolics

In the forest, laughter blooms,
Squirrels dance to nature's tunes.
With acorns flying, they play their game,
Who knew trees could join in the fame?

The brook babbles jokes in the sun,
As beavers chuckle, it's all in fun.
A deer trips over roots in delight,
Nature's giggles echo, what a sight!

Chatty birds gossip, branches sway,
While rabbits hop jokes all through the day.
What a blast in this woodland realm,
With humor reigning, we take the helm!

Under the moonlight, shadows prance,
Even owls join in this merry dance.
Laughter unites, the night is young,
In this forest of giggles, we've all just begun!

Fables Among the Firs

In the firs, a tale unfolds,
Of giggling gnomes and mischief bold.
A mushroom cap becomes a hat,
As trolls crack jokes from where they sat.

The wind whispers punchlines through the leaves,
While chipmunks chuckle, oh how it weaves!
Each sapling dreams of witty sights,
Creating laughter through the nights.

The wise old owl hoots a wisecrack,
While ants march forth, they won't hold back.
They share their stories, silly and bright,
In this woodland world of sheer delight.

Fables tangled in roots and grass,
Frogs tell jokes, oh, it's a blast!
Among the firs, the fun's never done,
For laughter blooms under the sun!

Joyful Sapling Shenanigans

Little saplings sway with glee,
Telling tales, as wild as can be.
One whispered, 'I'm taller than you!'
While another stuck out its tongue, too.

The gentle breeze joins in the jest,
As insects giggle, they do their best.
A squirrel stumbles, a dance gone wrong,
Yet each little fumble feels like a song.

In this playful patch of light and shade,
The laughter spreads, never to fade.
With sunshine beaming, and spirits high,
Each playful prank makes the moments fly.

They vow to spread joy through the wood,
With scritches and scratches, oh how they could!
Each joyful sapling spins and twirls,
Creating laughter that sweetly unfurls!

The Smirking Saplings

Amid the grove, the saplings grin,
With cheeky jokes shared among kin.
They whisper secrets of the dawn,
While stretching shadows, they laugh and yawn.

One smirked, 'I'm taller than you yesterday!'
The other shot back, 'You're a twig, hooray!'
Branches sway with playful boast,
As laughter ripples like a joyful host.

The sun dips low, a warm embrace,
Their comedy act, a merry chase.
With giggles rising, the air takes flight,
In this forest stage of pure delight.

As stars peek through, the fun won't cease,
Each smirking sapling brings forth peace.
With nature's humor, they shine anew,
In this woodland realm where laughter grew!

The Laughing Landscape

In the hills where shadows play,
Trees giggle as they sway.
Breezes carry silly sounds,
Nature's jest where joy abounds.

The daisies dance with glee,
Tickling toes in harmony.
Squirrels joke with acorn treats,
A comedy of furry feats.

Sunrise brings the chuckles bright,
Colors burst in pure delight.
Even clouds wear a grin so wide,
As laughter echoes through the tide.

In this place of joy and cheer,
Every moment's a souvenir.
So take a breath, let worries cease,
Join the fun, and feel the peace.

Aria of Laughter in the Pines

Among the pines where whispers roam,
Silly secrets find a home.
Branches sway in playful jest,
Nature's mirth, a charming quest.

A bird sings a tune so sweet,
While critters drum with tiny feet.
Rustling leaves share witty quips,
As sunlight dances, playfully skips.

The breeze tells tales of funny furs,
Of slippy slopes and bouncing furs.
Every tree embraces cheer,
In the forest, laughter's near.

So wander through this groovy scene,
Where humor reigns, it's evergreen.
Take a moment, laugh a while,
Let nature's whimsy make you smile.

Witty Woods' Whispers

In the woods where laughter flows,
Pine trees share the best of prose.
A squirrel chuckles, then a shout,
What's life without a little doubt?

Mushrooms giggle in their hats,
Frolicking with the chittering bats.
Hearts are light, the air is bright,
Witty woods bring pure delight.

Through the branches, jokes take flight,
Echoing in the starry night.
Every rustle is a clever scheme,
Nature's laughter is the theme.

So step into this charming scene,
Where jokes unfold like petals green.
Embrace the whimsy, take a chance,
Let the woods lead you in a dance.

The Enigma of Evergreen Giggles

In the green where laughter twirls,
Secrets hide in leafy swirls.
The trees shake with joyous glee,
Their giggles travel wild and free.

Each twig a joke, each leaf a pun,
Nature's humor weighing a ton.
Beneath the branches, chuckles bloom,
Drawing smiles in every room.

Rabbits hop with a playful tease,
Sharing tales that aim to please.
In this world, all worries flee,
With every laugh, we simply be.

So linger here, where fun's a trend,
In evergreen, the joy won't end.
Let echoes of giggles surround,
In this enchanted, funny ground.

Lighthearted in the Leafy Canopy

Up above, the branches sway,
Leaves giggle in a bright ballet.
A squirrel jokes with a cheeky grin,
"Who's making a nest? Where do I begin?"

The sun peeks through with a teasing flair,
And shadows dance with a flair so rare.
A caterpillar wears a tiny hat,
"I'm off to a party, how 'bout that?"

Beneath the tree, a rabbit hops high,
"Catch me if you can! Give it a try!"
But trip on roots, he tumbles with glee,
"Laughter's my game, just wait and see!"

And as twilight paints the sky o'erhead,
The fireflies glow, a twinkling thread.
Nature's comedy show comes alive,
In this leafy home, we thrive and jive.

The Hoax Among the Boughs

Once a wise owl spun tales at night,
Of treasures hidden, oh what a sight!
But when they searched with eager goals,
They found nothing but some lost shoals.

'It's all a ruse,' the old crow cawed,
While the squirrels snickered, all quite awed.
The truth revealed, laughter took flight,
In a game of jest 'neath the pale moonlight.

A raccoon pranks with mischief in mind,
Stealing shiny things, oh so unkind!
But when caught, he grins with sheer delight,
"Who doesn't love a good laugh at night?"

In the canopy's heart, mischief grows,
From rusty jokes to tickly toes.
Every branch holds a new surprise,
In the whispering woods, where humor lies.

Jovial Evergreen Stories

In the woods where the evergreens stand,
A bear tells tales, not quite as planned.
"I fought a moose!" he boasts with pride,
But all that happened was a slippery slide.

A witty fox rolls by with a grin,
"Did you hear about the pig that could swim?"
But when they checked, oh what a joke,
It was just a pig, dry as a smoke!

Frogs croak puns on lily pads near,
Their ribbits echo, full of cheer.
"Why jump so high? What's the big race?"
"Because we're just trying to lighten this place!"

As twilight falls on the green and the brown,
Laughter echoes, dispelling the frown.
With each tale spun under starlit skies,
The woods come alive with giggles and sighs.

Whispers of Woodland Whimsy

In the forest where laughter seems near,
A wise chipmunk whispers, "Come hear!"
"Why don't trees play hide and seek?"
"Because they're too rooted," he starts to speak.

A butterfly flutters, mischief in flight,
Tickling the noses of critters at night.
"Catch me if you can, oh what a dream!"
But they just giggle, it's a teamwork theme!

And the gnome with a grin, perched on the log,
Spins tales of a dance with a friendly fog.
"Beware of the mushrooms, they're tricky, you see!"
But under their caps, giggles grow free.

As shadows creep and stories unfold,
The woods chuckle softly, a sight to behold.
In this realm of whimsy, joy takes its flight,
With each whisper shared, the world feels just right.

Snappy Sprouts and Smiles

In the garden, sprouts declare,
"We're the snappiest, so beware!"
Leaves giggle, stretching wide,
As sunbeams join the merry ride.

Worms wiggle with a sly, sly grin,
"We turn compost into din!"
Buds burst out with cheer,
While ladybugs give a little leer.

The daisies gossip in the breeze,
"Who wore the best tonight, oh please?"
Bees buzz in with a joke to share,
"Honey's sweet, but laughter's rare!"

With every sprout, laughter grows,
In the garden, joy overflows.
Together we dance, together we sing,
In this happy place where giggles spring.

Chuckling in the Canopy

Up high in the leafy spree,
Squirrels quip, "Come climb with me!"
Branches bend with laughter's sway,
As birds make jokes throughout the day.

The wisdom of the owls takes flight,
"Who's the wisest? Me tonight!"
In shadows cast by moonlight's grace,
Each critter wears a cheeky face.

Raccoons rummage, giggling fun,
"We're the masters of moonlit run!"
While frogs croak in rhyming calls,
Creating echoes through the halls.

In the canopy, joy abounds,
With every laugh, the night resounds.
Under twinkling stars so bright,
We chuckle on till morning light.

Folklore of Forest Frolics

In the heart of the woody ground,
Whispers of humor all around.
Fairies giggle under their veils,
As they dance with mischievous trails.

A deer prances, hoofs on beat,
"I tell the stories, oh what a treat!"
With every flick of its ear,
The forest's secrets it will clear.

The mushrooms crow about their size,
"We're the stars under sunny skies!"
Bamboo bends, as if laughing too,
Joining in on the forest crew.

Legacy of jokes well spun,
In the forest, laughter's just begun.
Tales of old, lively and bright,
Bring joy to shadows, and light to night.

Wisecracks of the Wild

In the wild, where laughter springs,
Witty banter with curious things.
Chipmunks chuckle, acorns in paws,
"We're the rulers, hear our applause!"

A fox winks from behind a bush,
"Who said I can't in style, just hush!"
The wind whispers a clever jest,
As nature gives its very best.

Porcupines puff and say with flair,
"We poke fun, so do beware!"
And playful shadows dance on the ground,
With every giggle, joy is found.

From sunrise to the setting sun,
The wisecracks fly, and we all run.
In this wild realm, take a chance,
For laughter's the sweetest dance.

The Guffaws of Growth

In the forest where tall trees play,
A squirrel jokes, brightening the day.
With acorns tossed, he starts a game,
While laughing leaves whisper his name.

Roots intertwine, telling tales of old,
Of feisty winds and mischief bold.
A breeze that tickles branches high,
Turns serious trunks into a shy guy.

Fungi chuckle, sharing their spore,
As rabbits giggle, begging for more.
Nature's jesters, they all unite,
In this woodsy world, pure delight.

So if you listen, be keen and wise,
You'll catch the punches 'neath sunny skies.
Each giggle a sprout, each laugh a tree,
In the guffaws of growth, wild and free.

Trees with a Sense of Humor

Tall cedars crack jokes with the wind,
While chuckling leaves dance and spin.
A beech tree boasts of a tall tale,
  Of a squirrel who tried to sail.

Birches laugh with their bark so white,
  Sharing stories into the night.
A knotty oak, full of surprise,
Winks at the moon with a twinkling eye.

Pines whisper secrets, giggling loud,
Filling their branches, vibrant and proud.
Jokes about deer and their silly slips,
  With every chuckle, joyfully flips.

The canopy sways, in fits of glee,
Nature's humor, wild and carefree.
In a wood where laughter flows,
Trees are the jesters, as everyone knows.

Naughty Nature's Gags

A chipmunk sneaks into a picnic spread,
Swiping a crumb, then speeding ahead.
The ants all gossip, forming a queue,
Planning a raid, but giggling too.

Dandelions chuckle, sprouting in rows,
While sneaky weeds hide in garden clothes.
A wind-blown twig gives a playful poke,
Sending a ripple of laughter to stoke.

The sun peeks out with a mischievous grin,
Warming the earth for the chaos within.
Berry bushes hold secrets galore,
Tickling berries that burst with a roar.

In nature's realm where pranks are bright,
Joy springs forth, like a punchline in flight.
Every rustle, every breeze,
Brings forth laughter among the trees.

The Enchanted Laughter of Pines

Underneath boughs where shadows blend,
Sprightly whispers seem to extend.
A pine tree giggles, swaying with flair,
Spreading spiky jokes on the air.

The forest floor chuckles with ticks,
As critters slip in their playful tricks.
Mossy carpets, lush and bright,
Echo the laughter that dances in light.

With needles sharp, and wisdom vast,
Pine humor travels, unsurpassed.
Every tree's tale, a quirky jest,
A giggle that puts nature to the test.

So listen close when you wander through,
In this realm of green, laughter is true.
With the enchanted, merry and kind,
Finding joy in nature, the heart aligned.

The Sassy Sapling Saga

In the grove, a sapling sings,
With jokes that flap like tiny wings,
It cracks a smile on every face,
As laughter spreads through every space.

A squirrel stops to catch the jest,
While birds in chorus do their best,
To chirp along with every pun,
In this green realm, the joy is fun!

A breeze arrives, it tickles trees,
Sassy sounds and giggles tease,
As branches sway to nature's tune,
The sapling sparkles like a moon.

With beetles laughing, fuzzy ants,
Join in the craziness and dance,
In this tale of joy and cheer,
The sassy sapling holds us near.

Clever Cones and Comical Currents

A clever cone with sharp wit shines,
Tells tales of roots and tangled lines,
It rolls away, but not too far,
Its humor spreads like a shooting star.

In the shade of giant trees,
Laughter twirls upon the breeze,
With every nudge and playful shove,
They tease and joke, with so much love.

A chipmunk joins the frolic cheer,
With nutty puns that we all hear,
The piney crowd is often loud,
As giggles dance, they're feeling proud.

As daylight fades in soft delight,
The clever cones bring joy to night,
Around the trunk, they form a ring,
And laugh until the moon takes wing.

Humor in the Forest Shadows

In shadows where the forest plays,
A fox recounts its funny ways,
With puns that make the night seem bright,
And whispers carried by the night.

The owls, wise with comic eyes,
Share quirks of trees and cheeky lies,
As crickets join in joyous song,
Where laughter proves we all belong.

A hedgehog brings a rolling joke,
With quills that spark a playful poke,
While fireflies wink in merry dances,
Creating sparkles through their prances.

In shadows deep, the fun runs free,
As nature hosts a jubilee,
And every nook and cranny knows,
That humor here forever grows.

The Lighthearted Life of Limbs

Old limbs stretch out with tales to tell,
Of laughter echoing like a bell,
With every rustle, tickles rise,
Beneath the vast and open skies.

Twisted trunks share silly lore,
Of playful winds and branches soar,
As woodland friends all gather 'round,
In joy and warmth, they all are found.

A jolly squirrel wears a grin,
While leaves applaud the fun within,
With every shake and jive anew,
The lively limbs dance on cue.

In this lighthearted, leafy space,
They spin the jokes with such good grace,
For in the grove, as night appears,
Laughter fills the forest's gears.

Whispers of the Woodland Wit

In the forest where the trees confide,
Squirrels gossip, nowhere to hide.
Barking trees with a voice so spry,
Crack jokes as they wave their boughs up high.

Beneath the canopy, shadows play,
Frogs croak punchlines, adding to the fray.
Each acorn drops with a little cheer,
Nature's laughter ringing loud and clear.

Rabbits dance in dappled light,
Telling tales of their manic flight.
Their hops and skips, a comic sight,
As birds chirp quips from their lofty height.

In the woodland, mirth does bloom,
Every rustle feels like a boom.
Giggles echo beneath the sun,
Where laughter's woven, side by side, in fun.

Quips from the Coniferous Canopy

Up in the pines, a jester took flight,
With pine needles sharp and spirits bright.
He tickled the branches, made the sap dance,
Every chuckle a cheeky chance.

The owls hoot riddles, wise and sly,
While woodpeckers drum, oh so spry.
Each beat a punchline, crisp and clear,
In the shade of the branches, laughter draws near.

Caterpillars giggle on leaves so green,
Sharing secrets that must not be seen.
They munch away while telling a joke,
In a world where both silence and humor provoke.

Amidst the towering trunks, silly tales unfold,
With every whisper, more jokes we're told.
Nature's laughter swirls through the air,
In a canopy of giggles, we happily share.

Jests Among the Needles

In the thicket, mischief brews,
With pinecones plotting their playful dues.
A chipmunk chuckles at the fumbled heaps,
As tall firs sway and tickle the creeps.

A bearded man in a tree stump sits,
Telling stories with jester fits.
With every twist of his whiskered grin,
The forest roars, where humor begins.

While deer pass by with a curious glance,
They trip in the underbrush, it's quite the dance.
Each slip gets met with a boisterous cheer,
As laughter sprinkles like sunshine here.

Jests flicker through the branches so vast,
In this playful grove, the fun's unsurpassed.
Nature's comedians take to the stage,
Where jokes and giggles will never age.

The Arborist's Amusement

An arborist winks with a twinkling eye,
As saplings wiggle, passing jokes by.
With trowels and shovels, they dig and delight,
Hilarity grows in gardens so bright.

A garden gnome shares his silliest tales,
Of critters that dance and wind-blown sails.
Soap bubbles float as he laughs with glee,
Creating fizzles in the greenery.

On pathways woven with petals so sweet,
Each flower gabs with a sassy beat.
Bees buzz by with their buzzing schtick,
For every bloom, there's a silly trick.

As shadows stretch with the setting sun,
The laughter ripples, a daily run.
In nature's embrace, we chuckle and smile,
Each moment's a punchline, full of style.

Giggles in the Greenery

In a forest so bright, a squirrel took flight,
Chasing his tail, oh what a sight!
He tripped on a root, fell flat with a thud,
Left giggles behind, all muddy with mud.

A bear painted nails, quite a bold feat,
He wore them with pride, oh isn't that sweet?
The bees buzzing loudly, they couldn't believe,
Nature's own fashion? Oh, who would conceive!

A rabbit named Charlie wore glasses so round,
Complaining about carrots that weren't quite profound.
His friends had a laugh, it echoed and soared,
When he tried to hop high, his feet got ignored.

With chipmunks who sing in a silly grand way,
Their acorn band jams throughout the day.
Leave worry behind, let joy take its place,
In greenery's giggles, we find our true grace.

Witty Whispers from the Woods

A wise old owl hooted jokes from the tree,
His audience laughed, oh it's plain to see.
A raccoon with quirks, wearing socks with a flair,
He danced on the logs, in the sun's morning glare.

Leaves whispered secrets of squirrels and grubs,
As lumbering turtles shared quite the fun jubs.
A hedgehog with wit threw a pun that went,
Rolling downhill, a real giggle event!

Deer pranced around in a curious way,
Tripping on branches, oh what a display!
With laughter so light, it floated on air,
Witty whispers grew jovial everywhere.

In shadows and sun, joyous spirits would roam,
Telling tall tales, making woods feel like home.
Nature's own jesters, in bright colors gleamed,
In the heart of the woods, all humor redeemed.

The Humor of Hidden Hollows

In a hollow so snug, lived a fox with a grin,
Always up to antics, a mischievous win.
He turned grapes to jelly, and jelly to jam,
Then licked his own paws, saying, "Oh, what a slam!"

The raccoons joined in, with their dancing parade,
Crafting costumes from leaves that nature had laid.
They twirled 'round the glade with a flair quite divine,
Laughing at fireflies who flickered in line.

A squirrel named Max preached wisdom in jest,
Telling all his friends that laughter's the best.
With each little joke, he cracked up the crew,
In those hidden hollows, joy really grew.

So raise your acorns, toast to the mirth,
For humor and friendship are treasures of worth.
In the shade of the trees, where giggles collide,
We share in the laughter, the fun we can't hide.

Lighthearted Leafy Lore

In a realm of green where the chuckles abound,
A turtle recited some jokes that astound.
He slipped on a leaf and slid all around,
The laughter erupted, oh what a sound!

A snail with a violin played tunes so sweet,
While crickets kept time with their delicate feet.
With critters all cheering in joyful delight,
The forest united in laughter that night.

An ant told a tale of a berry so bold,
It danced on the vine, in stories retold.
His friends held their bellies, they laughed till they cried,
In the leafy lore, where joy simply can't hide.

So gather together 'neath branches so wide,
Savoring moments where humor can glide.
In life's leafy lessons, let laughter be core,
For lighthearted spirits will always add more.

Frivolous Forest Tales

In the woods where critters play,
A dance-off starts at break of day.
Squirrels strut, with style and flair,
Who knew they'd rock the forest fair?

The owl hoots jokes so wise and bold,
While bunnies hop as tales unfold.
They giggle at trees that sway and bend,
Creating laughter that knows no end.

A raccoon juggles acorns bright,
While frogs croak puns by moonlight.
Each rustling leaf a quip or pun,
In this forest, humor's never done.

So let's wander through this merry land,
With laughter echoing, oh so grand.
For every twist and every turn,
Hold tight to joy, let your heart burn.

Giggling Under the Canopy

Beneath the leaves, where sunlight streams,
Giggling creatures share their dreams.
A chipmunk spins a tale so tall,
While echoes of laughter bounce off the wall.

The branches sway, it's quite a sight,
As the parrot cracks jokes in flight.
"Feathered friends, this is no jest!"
With giggles, they all feel quite blessed.

The turtle chuckles, slow but wise,
While fireflies blink like little eyes.
"Why rush?" he says, with a grin so wide,
"Life's a joyride, come enjoy the ride!"

So under the canopy, join the fun,
In fields of laughter, we all run.
For every quirky twist of fate,
Brings giggles galore, oh so great.

Pines And Puns

Among the pines, a gathering's set,
Where laughter and puns are truly met.
A hedgehog tells tales of great delight,
While the sun dips low and stars shine bright.

"Why do the squirrels never share?"
"Because they're nuts!" they all declare.
The thumping feet of rabbits near,
Spread funny tales and joyful cheer.

The tall pine trees sway with ease,
"Hey buddy, don't forget to sneeze!"
They poke fun at the passing breeze,
Leaving laughter hanging like leaves on trees.

So gather round, don't miss the fun,
In this lilting grove, joy's never done.
Where every bark and every grin,
Brings puns galore, let joy begin.

Nature's Comedic Roots

Down in the roots where laughter grows,
A funny tale everyone knows.
The mushrooms giggle, their caps held high,
As insects dance, oh me, oh my!

"Why did the tree refuse to speak?"
"Because it felt barked at all week!"
The ferns sway gently in delight,
Echoing jokes under the moonlight.

A wise old oak with stories vast,
Tells of mishaps that left them aghast.
With every twist and turn of fate,
He proves that laughter conquers hate.

So dive into roots of humor deep,
Where nature's laughter makes hearts leap.
In this realm where joy takes flight,
Hold tight to giggles, morning to night.

Jestful Journeys through Green Tapestry

In the forest, squirrels dance around,
Telling tales of acorns they've found.
With a wink and a nod, they scurry with glee,
Their laughter, a melody, wild and free.

A rabbit hops by, wearing a hat,
Tripped on a twig, oh, imagine that!
He shakes off the leaves with a comical flair,
And all of the critters just stop and stare.

Owl in the oak chuckles loud and clear,
'Who needs a party? Just bring some cheer!'
With a wink of his eye and a swoosh of his wing,
Nature's own jester, he rules everything.

So stroll through the green with a laugh on your face,
Nature's a stage, and it's full of grace.
Every twist and turn brings a surprise or two,
In this tapestry where mirth is the view.

Gags from the Green Glade.

Under the shade, where the wildflowers play,
A frog cracks a joke, brightening the day.
He leaps with a grin, hops right into a puddle,
Splashing all around, oh, what a muddle!

The hedgehog, quite clever, rolls into a ball,
Says, 'I'm just a burrito, I'm ready for a fall!'
With laughter erupting from skies above,
Even the bees buzz with chuckles of love.

A wise old chair, where the mice like to dwell,
Holds secrets of giggles they dare not tell.
With every tiny nibble and sneak of a snack,
They add to the humor—we can't hold it back!

So gather around in the glade of delight,
Where whimsy and gags fill the air every night.
With nature's own jokes sprouting fresh from the earth,
Laughter and joy reign, for all of their worth.

Nature's Quirky Jests

A dandelion puff whispers in the breeze,
'Sneezing is fun, but don't forget to sneeze!'
With every petal that floats to the ground,
Nature's own humor can always be found.

The clouds play tag in a sky painted bright,
Shifting and drifting, what a funny sight!
A chubby old bear swings from a tree,
He lands with a thud, 'Guess it's just me!'

The fish in the brook wear smirks on their scales,
As they practice their jumps and tell silly tales.
They flip and they splash, with each playful swish,
Nature's comedy show—let's all make a wish!

With giggles and chuckles, the green world runs,
From blossoms to branches, it's brimming with fun.
So take a deep breath and enjoy every jest,
In the land of the quirky, we're truly blessed.

The Whimsical Seedlings

Tiny green sprouts peek from the ground,
Whispering secrets, so joyful, profound.
They'd sway to the rhythm of breeze and of fun,
Creating a party under the sun.

A beetle in stripes struts around with pride,
Says, 'Join in my march, there's laughter inside!'
With every small step, every shuffle makes light,
The world is a dance floor, come join in the flight!

A blushing tomato, quite shy of the crew,
Said, 'I'd tell a joke, but I'm feeling too blue!'
Then burst into laughter, bright colors ablaze,
Even her giggle stems sprouted a gaze.

So cherish those seedlings, each quirky delight,
Their antics remind us to laugh day and night.
In the garden of whimsy, find joy in the small,
For nature's own laughter is the best joy of all.

The Mirthful Museum of Pines

In a hall of wooden laughter,
Tree trunks dance with goofy glee.
Acorns play the jester's part,
Leaves tickle with a whispery plea.

A squirrel dons a comical hat,
Telling tales of nutty schemes.
The bark cracks jokes, a little flat,
But spreads smiles like sunny beams.

Saplings giggle, stretching tall,
Pretending they're the tallest trees.
In this museum, fun's the call,
Nature's humor floats on breeze.

So come and join this leafy fun,
Where laughter blooms among the pines.
Each tree a joker, every pun,
In this quirky, green design.

Cackles in the Canopy

Above the ground, in leafy nooks,
Chirping birds share silly tales.
A wise old owl reads comic books,
While giggling squirrels hit the trails.

Branches sway with jests and tricks,
Tickling the clouds with their pranks.
Raccoons share their favorite flicks,
Plotting mischief in the ranks.

Rustling leaves join in the jest,
Echoing with giggling cheer.
Nature's stage, it's simply blessed,
With laughter ringing loud and clear.

So peek above, let joy take flight,
In this canopy of cheer.
With every chortle, day is bright,
A world alive, where laughter's near.

The Joyful Sylva

In this wood of endless cheer,
Trees wear grins, their spirits bright.
Each creature spins a tale sincere,
With giggles that take flight.

Frogs play leapfrog, frogs take note,
While wooden beams embrace the fun.
A raccoon juggles with a gloat,
Beneath the beaming midday sun.

Breezes whisper jokes untold,
Rustling through the laughing crowd.
Every wisp a punchline bold,
Sprouting giggles, fierce and loud.

So trod the path with glee today,
Join in this woodland dance divine.
Let humor lead and guide your way,
In the joyful sylva, let love shine.

Tongue-in-Cheek Twigs

Little twigs with cheeky flair,
Bend and twist in playful style.
They share puns upon the air,
    Living up to every smile.

Boughs band together for a show,
Cracking jokes that tickle the heart.
With every sway, they steal the show,
    Nature's humor, a fine art.

The wind whispers witty banter,
While bushes blush in green delight.
Each leaf a comedian, a canter,
    Making giggling hearts feel light.

So leap with joy from twig to twig,
    In this forest of pure mirth.
With laughter big and moments big,
    Find comic gold in nature's girth.

www.ingramcontent.com/pod-product-compliance
Lightning Source LLC
Chambersburg PA
CBHW072146200426
43209CB00051B/789